Searchlight BOOKS™

Spy Secrets

Secret Spy Skills

Christy Peterson

Lerner Publications ◆ Minneapolis

Lerner Publications Company
An imprint of Lerner Publishing Group, Inc.
241 First Avenue North
Minneapolis, MN 55401 USA

For reading levels and more information, look up this title at www.lernerbooks.com.

Main body text set in Adrianna Regular.
Typeface provided by Chank.

Editor: Shee Yang **Designer:** Mary Ross

Library of Congress Cataloging-in-Publication Data

Names: Peterson, Christy, author.
Title: Secret spy skills / Christy Peterson.
Description: Minneapolis : Lerner Publications, [2021] | Series: Searchlight books- spy secrets | Includes bibliographical references and index. | Audience: Ages 8–11 | Audience: Grades 2–3 | Summary: "Being a political spy can be a very dangerous job. From undercover work to wire-tapping, readers will learn all about espionage and the spies of the political underworld"— Provided by publisher.
Identifiers: LCCN 2020009474 (print) | LCCN 2020009475 (ebook) | ISBN 9781728404264 (library binding) | ISBN 9781728418681 (ebook)
Subjects: LCSH: Espionage—Juvenile literature. | Spies—Juvenile literature. | Intelligence service—Juvenile literature.
Classification: LCC JF1525.I6 P4792 2021 (print) | LCC JF1525.I6 (ebook) | DDC 327.12—dc23

LC record available at https://lccn.loc.gov/2020009474
LC ebook record available at https://lccn.loc.gov/2020009475

Manufactured in the United States of America
1-48484-48998-8/21/2020

Table of Contents

Chapter 1

WHEN SECRETS CHANGE HISTORY

During the American Civil War (1861–1865), military strength was the key to victory. The Confederate and Union armies were each working to build a new type of weapon for themselves: a warship armored in iron. The Union intelligence didn't know that the Confederate army had stolen parts of a Union warship, the USS *Merrimack*, to build their new and improved weapon. They were nearly finished building their own ironclad ship, the CSS *Virginia*.

The Confederate and Union armies used warships in the Civil War.

A freed slave named Marie Louvestre was working for the Confederate engineer who was building the *Virginia*. When Louvestre overheard the details of the *Virginia*, she knew the breakthrough could change the outcome of the war. She stole copies of the plans and walked 200 miles (322 km) north to where the Union army was stationed. Louvestre met with a Union leader and handed over the plans.

The Battle of Hampton Road, also known as the Battle of *Monitor* and *Merrimack*, was a battle between warships in the Civil War.

The Union had no idea the *Virginia* was nearly completed. They wouldn't be able to destroy the ship before it launched. But Louvestre's information helped the Union prepare for the incoming battle.

Why Spy?

The more a government knows, the more easily it can keep people safe. That's why government agencies secretly collect information about other countries and groups. Agencies collect all kinds of secret information, also called intelligence.

Spy agencies are always collecting information.

Meet a Spy!

During the Revolutionary War (1775–1783), James Armistead Lafayette, a Virginian slave, was permitted by his master to spy on the British. Pretending to be an escaped slave, Lafayette infiltrated British troops and helped them navigate the Virginian wilderness while he gathered intelligence for the Americans.

After being notified by Lafayette of a surprise attack from the enemy, the American troops were able to plan a successful defense. Lafayette's greatest contribution is the Battle of Yorktown (September 28, 1781–October 19, 1781). It was the final major land battle of the Revolutionary War.

Spies use technology to gather information during surveillance.

One of the ways spies gather intelligence is through surveillance. Surveillance can be as simple as listening in on a conversation or as complicated as tracking the movements of a general in another country. Using technology, spies can conduct surveillance from nearly any distance or location.

Chapter 2

BLENDING IN

In movies, government spies are nearly superhuman. They can fight off bad guys using their wits, charm, or latest spy gadgets. And they do it all alone. In reality, spying takes a team, and every member of the team plays an important role.

It Takes a Team

A government spy is an agent. Before a spy is recruited to be an agent, handlers consider a number of things, including how well an agent can blend in. Handlers often recruit spies from targeted communities. For example, a police officer could be recruited by a handler to look into police corruption at his station.

Agents receive instructions from and report to their handler. Once the handler collects enough information, the handler reports it back to the spy agency.

Agents and handlers work together to help get intelligence for their spy agency.

Back at the agency, a team of carefully selected specialists studies the information. They use the intelligence gathered to make recommendations about what to do next. Sometimes agencies in one country will also work together with agencies in another country. They share secrets to keep people safe.

A SPY AGENCY REVIEWS GATHERED INTELLIGENCE.

Spies often use fake identities during missions.

Unlike movie spies, agents and handlers have to blend in. Keeping a low profile is an important part of spying. Agents often use covers, or fake identities. Agents are given counterfeit documents such as passports, birth certificates, and driver's licenses. Their covers sometimes include made-up life stories. Handlers will give their spies new birthdays, names, and even childhood memories. Sometimes two spies will pretend to be a couple to seem more ordinary.

Chapter 3

WAITING AND WATCHING

An agency will sometimes place a sleeper agent in a location they want to collect information about. A sleeper agent is a spy who appears to live an ordinary life. They lay low until their handler tells them to make a move. The Federal Bureau of Investigation (FBI), a government spy agency, thought this was the case with a man named Chi Mak.

Mak immigrated to the US from China. For twenty years, Mak worked as an engineer for a military company with direct ties to the US Navy. Around 2004, the FBI heard that someone might be stealing plans from the company where Mak worked and delivering them to China. They began to suspect Mak due to his position at the company. The FBI set up an investigation.

The FBI believed Mak was sending US naval secrets to China.

That's a Fact!

In 1945, children in the Soviet Union (a former nation of republics that included Russia) gifted the US ambassador with a large wood carving. The gift seemed to be a sign of goodwill between the two countries, and it hung in the ambassador's office for years. But the carving held a secret. The US State Department eventually discovered a bug hidden inside the carving. A bug is a device that secretly records conversations. Soviet spies had been listening to the US ambassador from a car parked across the street.

Secrets in the Trash

The FBI began to spy on Mak. To find evidence, they bugged Mak's home and office. They set up surveillance outside his house and went through Mak's trash. While Mak and his wife were away on vacation, the FBI entered their home.

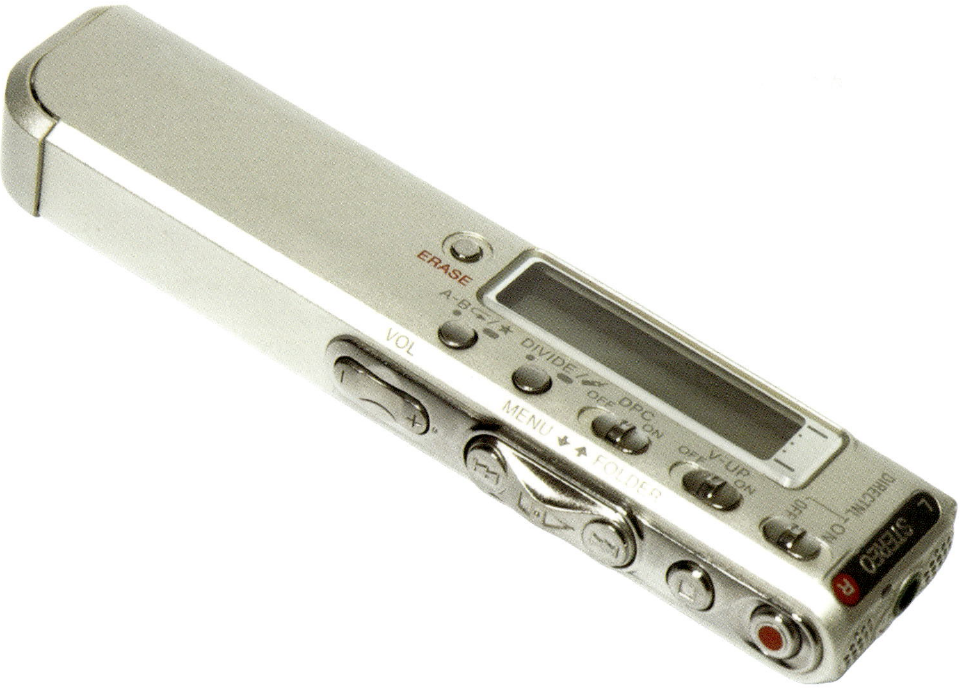

SPIES OFTEN USE RECORDERS TO CAPTURE CONVERSATIONS.

Papers with important information were found all over Mak's house.

The FBI found the house covered in dust. Throughout the house were piles of paper with sensitive information but nothing that proved Mak was a spy. Wherever they disturbed the dust, FBI agents applied dust to the area so Mak would not know they had been inside his house.

The months of carefully looking through Mak's trash finally paid off. An agent discovered small pieces of a torn-up paper. The agent collected all the pieces found and worked to put them back together. The paper turned out to be a tasking list—a set of directions from a handler. The agents also discovered another tasking list with instructions on how to sneak the information back to China.

The FBI combed through Mak's trash for evidence.

But the tasking lists were not enough evidence. The FBI snuck back into Mak's house and hid a video camera. They filmed Mak and his wife saving files onto a disk. The FBI agents were patient. They needed concrete evidence to convict Mak of spying for China. They waited to see what Mak would do with the disk.

HIDDEN VIDEO CAMERAS CAN CAPTURE EVIDENCE.

Mak saved important files on a disk.

Mak met with his brother and handed over the disk. The FBI found out that Mak's brother and sister-in-law would be going to China. The agents waited until the couple arrived at the airport.

The FBI finally made their move. The disk was seized and analyzed. It was an encrypted file that contained information about a new submarine engine. Mak was not authorized to share this navy technology with China. The FBI arrested Mak, his brother, and their wives. Mak was sentenced to twenty-four years in prison.

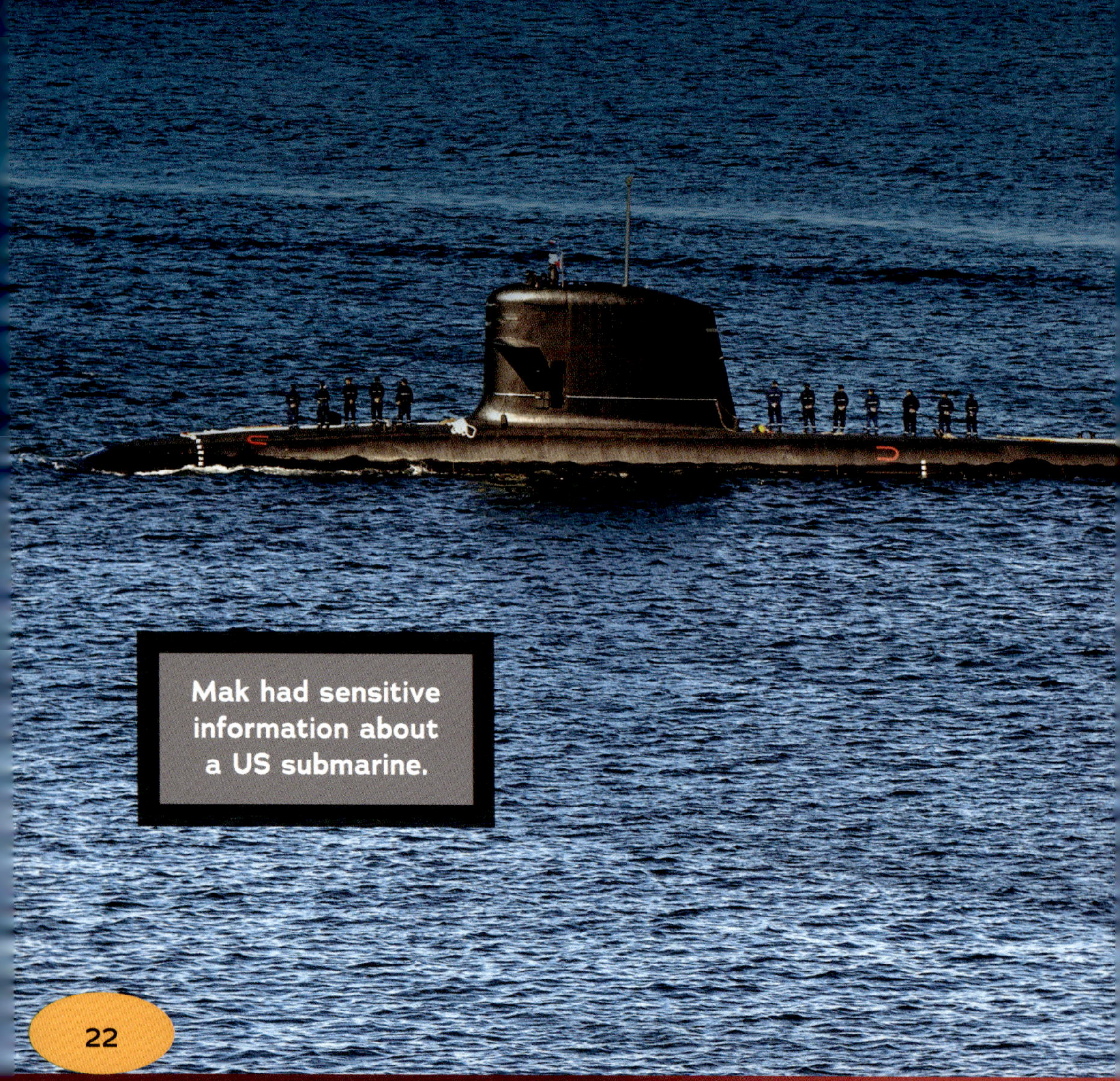

Mak had sensitive information about a US submarine.

Chapter 4

EYES EVERYWHERE

The Mak case involved careful, close-up surveillance. But spy agencies also use tools flying far overhead to spy on countries and individuals. Farthest up are spy satellites. These machines circle Earth in space. The cameras on a spy satellite are powerful. They can spot something as small as a basketball in a backyard.

MILITARY SURVEILLANCE DRONES FLY OVER ENEMY TERRITORY.

Countries also use spy planes. These planes fly so high that they are hard to detect. But even the highest, fastest spy planes can be shot down. So, many agencies use drones to fly over enemy territory. Drones are flown by remote control. The pilots can be thousands of miles away. This keeps pilots safe while their drones collect useful intelligence.

That's a Fact!

Planes weren't the first spy tools to take to the air. During the Civil War, spies rose into the sky in balloons. Strong ropes attached the balloons to the ground or a ship. Hundreds of feet above the battlefield, a balloon pilot could report the exact position of the enemy.

Of course, the balloons weren't very sneaky. The enemy could easily spot them. But the balloons could be used to help generals map out large areas of unknown territory to plan attack and defense strategies.

High-Tech Spying

Technology has opened up many new ways to gather intelligence. Cell phones fill the pockets of millions of people around the world. Tracking someone has never been easier. Spies can track their target's movements using cell towers. They can hack into the target's cell phone and listen in on conversations or read text messages.

Governments also spy on their citizens. In 2013, a Central Intelligence Agency (CIA) employee leaked evidence that the National Security Agency (NSA), an official office of the US Department of Defense, has been monitoring millions of people through their cell phones.

Spies can track their targets through the target's cell phone.

But modern tools can also make spying harder. For example, finding out on the internet about someone's past is easy. So it's much harder to create a convincing cover.

Spying will always be a game of outwitting the other side. And agencies will keep coming up with new ways to uncover secrets and give their side an advantage.

Spy agencies are always developing new ways to find information.

I Spy!

One of the most important skills a spy can have is a good memory. Agents have to be able to recall details about their covers as well as secret instructions that cannot be written down. A good memory can keep agents safe and make their missions successful.

You can improve your memory by playing a simple game. Have a friend pick ten objects, and place them in a box or under a towel. Uncover the items for thirty seconds, and study each one. Then cover them again and see how many you can remember.

Glossary

agency: an organization that collects and analyzes secret information

agent: a person who steals secret information and passes it along to a spy agency

Confederate: states in the South that wanted to keep slavery and split America into two countries during the Civil War

counterfeit: an imitation of something valuable such as money or government badges

cover: a secret identity

handler: a person who hires and manages spies on behalf of a spy agency

intelligence: the collection of information about an enemy, a possible enemy, or an area

sleeper agent: an agent that lives and works in a place for a period before beginning to spy

surveillance: watching and listening to gather information

tasking list: a list of information to steal

Union: states in the North that wanted to reunite America during the Civil War

Learn More

Alberti, Enigma. *Mary Bowser and the Civil War Spy Ring.* New York: Workman, 2017.

American Battlefield Trust: Civil War Ballooning
https://www.battlefields.org/learn/galleries/civil-war-ballooning

Central Intelligence Agency: Spy Kids
https://www.cia.gov/kids-page/

International Spy Museum: "Language of Espionage"
https://www.spymuseum.org/education-programs/spy-resources/language-of-espionage/

Peterson, Christy. *Secret Spy Hacks.* Minneapolis: Lerner Publications, 2021.

Rockwell, Anne. *A Spy Called James: The True Story of James Lafayette, Revolutionary War Double Agent.* Minneapolis: Carolrhoda Books, 2016.

Index

Photo Acknowledgments

Image credits: Matthew Brady/Wikimedia Commons (public domain), p. 5; Buyenlarge/Getty Images, p. 6; Octa corp/Shutterstock.com, p. 7; Virginia Historical Society image/Wikimedia Commons (public domain), p. 8; Andrey_Popov/Shutterstock.com, p. 9; Pressmaster/Shutterstock.com, p. 11; OneStockPhoto/Shutterstock.com, p. 12; Olivier Le Queinec/Shutterstock.com, p. 13; Kanok Sulaiman/Shutterstock.com, p. 15; Alexey D. Vedernikov/Shutterstock.com, p. 17; Billion Photos/Shutterstock.com, p. 18; Clow Clerm Club/Shutterstock.com, p. 19; FUN FUN PHOTO/Shutterstock.com, p. 20; photosthai/Shutterstock.com, p. 21; byvalet/Shutterstock.com, p. 22; sibsky2016/Shutterstock.com, p. 24; Library of Congress (LC-USZ62-56907), p. 25; ZoFot/Shutterstock.com, pp. 26–27; Nomad_Soul/Shutterstock.com, p. 28.

Cover: Stokkete/Shutterstock.com.